Mathematics 3
Problem Solving Activities

Wendy Klassen

Editorial Advisor
Doug Super

Project Editor
Fran Seidenberg

DISTRIBUTOR

DALE SEYMOUR PUBLICATIONS
P.O. BOX 10888
PALO ALTO, CA 94303

Order Number DS01527
ISBN 0-86651-254-3
(previously ISBN 0-395-33020-3)
  cdefghi-MA-8932109

DALE
SEYMOUR
PUBLICATIONS
P.O. BOX 10888
PALO ALTO, CA 94303

CONTENTS

UNIT 1 Sorting and Classifying

Which one does *not* belong? Print **a**, **b**, **c**, or **d**.

1.

2.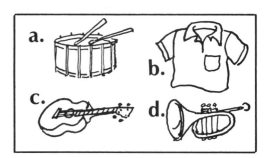

3.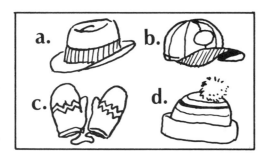

4.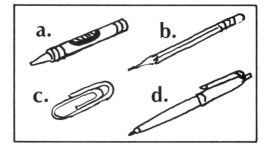

5.

6.

7.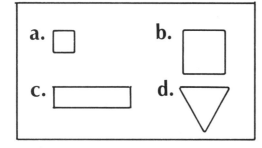

8.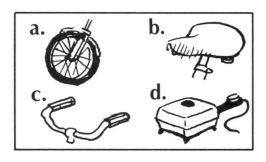

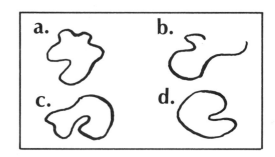

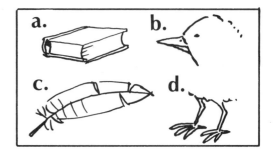

Which one belongs? Print the letter.

1.

a.

2.

b.

3.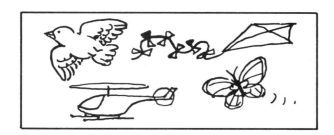

c.

d.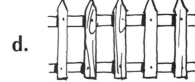

4.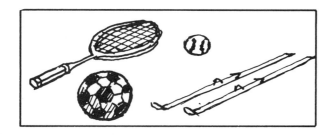

e.

5.

f.

Which one belongs? Print **a**, **b**, **c**, or **d**.

1. The letter has torn.
   Which do you need to fix the letter?

   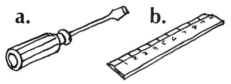

   a.   **b.**   **c.**   **d.**

2. The tea is getting cold.
   Which does the teapot need?

   a. **b.** **c.**  **d.**

3. The girl's bangs are too long.
   Which do you need to make them shorter?

   a.  **b.**  **c.**  **d.**

4. The stool is too long.
   Which do you need to make it shorter?

   a. **b.**  **c.**  **d.**

5. The fruit is too high.
   Which do you need to get the fruit?

   a. 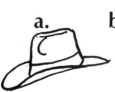 **b.**  **c.**  **d.**

Which one does *not* belong?

1. You want to bake a cake.
   Which does not belong?

   a. b. c. d.

2. You want to do your homework.
   Which does not belong?

   a. b. c. d.

3. You want to sew on a button.
   Which does not belong?

   a. b. c. d.

4. You want to wash the car.
   Which does not belong?

   a. b. c. d.

5. You want to make a fort.
   Which does not belong?

   a. b. c. d.

UNIT 2   Reading Stories

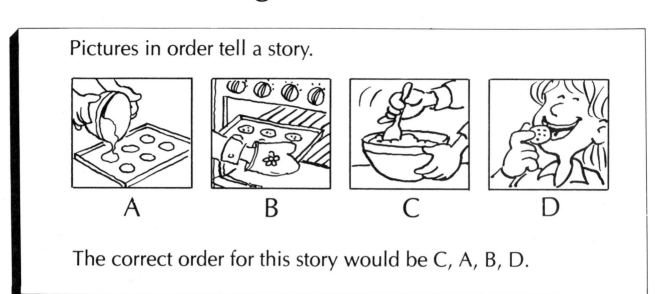

Pictures in order tell a story.

A   B   C   D

The correct order for this story would be C, A, B, D.

Put the pictures in order.

1.   A   B   C   D

2.   A   B   C   D

3.   A   B   C   D

The pictures tell a story. Put them in order.

1.
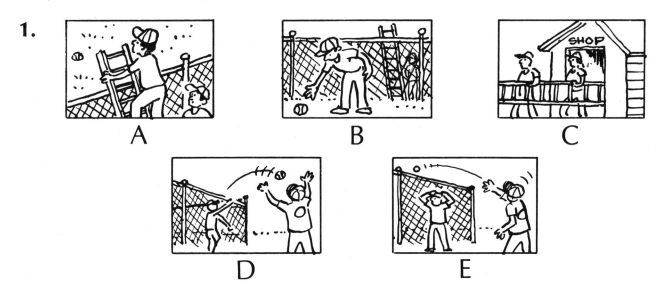

2. Which comes first?

3. Which comes third?

4. When does picture A come in the story?

5.

6. Which comes first?

7. Which comes third?

8. Which comes sixth?

9. Which comes last?

10. When does picture A come in the story?

Which picture matches the story? Print the letter.

1. 12 cookies
   8 are eaten.
   How many are left?

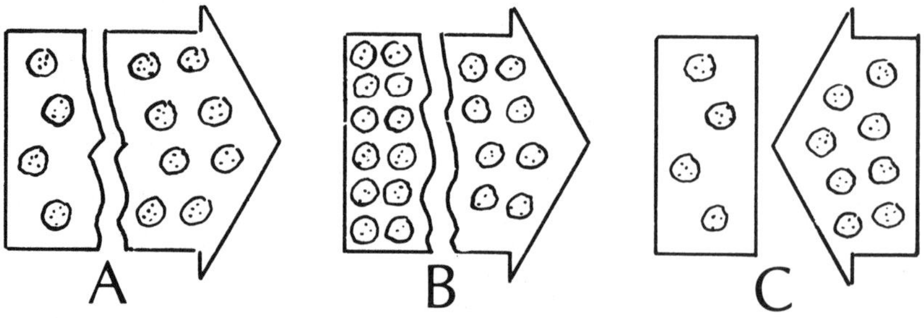

   A   B   C

2. 6 snails join
   9 fish.
   How many animals?

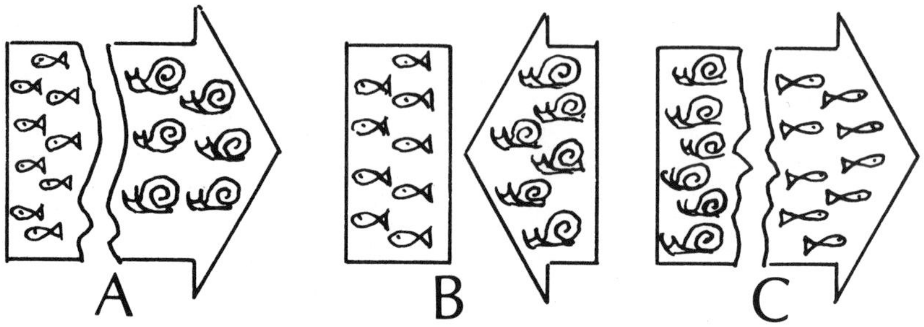

   A   B   C

3. 7 boys in all
   5 go home.
   How many are left?

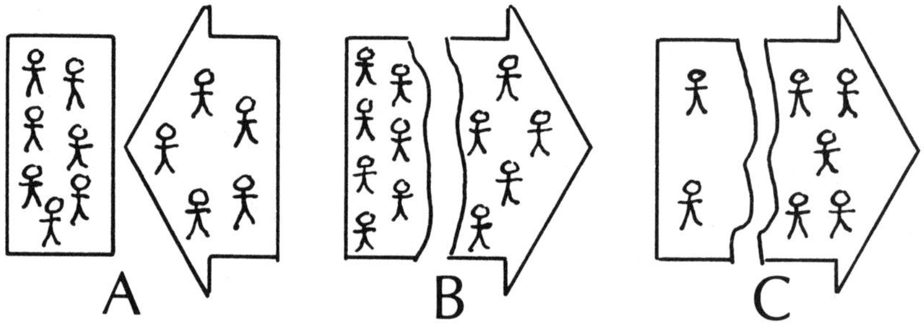

   A   B   C

4. 4 ants
   9 more come.
   How many now?

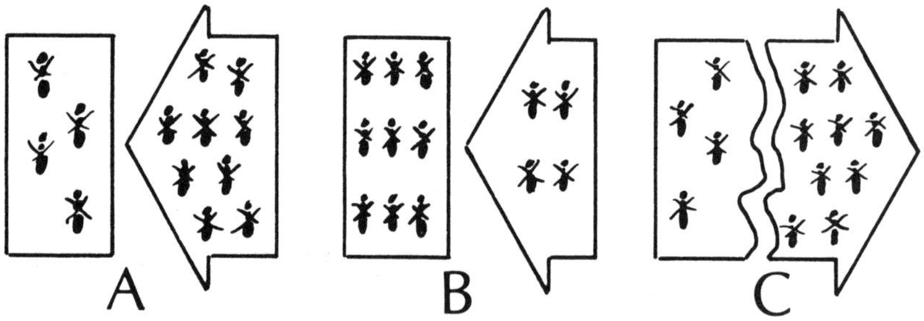

   A   B   C

5. 14 keys at first
   6 are lost.
   How many are left?

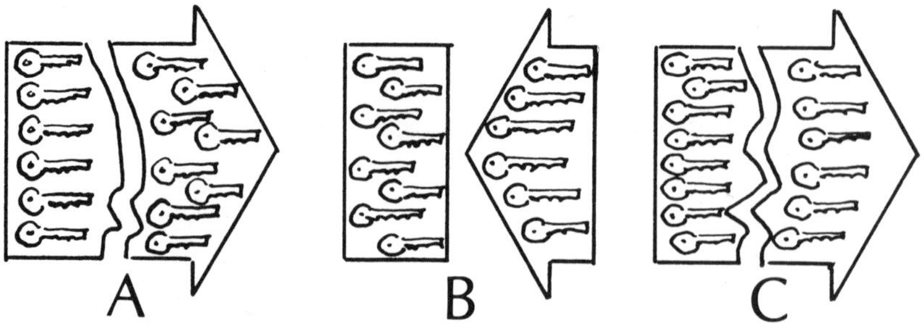

   A   B   C

Read the story. Answer the questions.

CIRCUS PARADE

The Big Top Circus came to town last weekend. There was a parade. The 6 elephants and 8 white horses were the largest animals in the parade. A girl rode on top of each elephant and horse.

Six acrobats did headstands and other tricks along the way. Three dogs jumped through a hoop held by their trainer.

Best of all were the 4 clowns. They each had one little monkey on their arm. Everyone liked them.

1. How many large animals?

2. How many small animals?

3. How many animals in all?

4. How many girls rode on top of an elephant or horse?

5. How many people were in the parade?

UNIT 3   Geometry Patterns

Draw the two figures that come next.

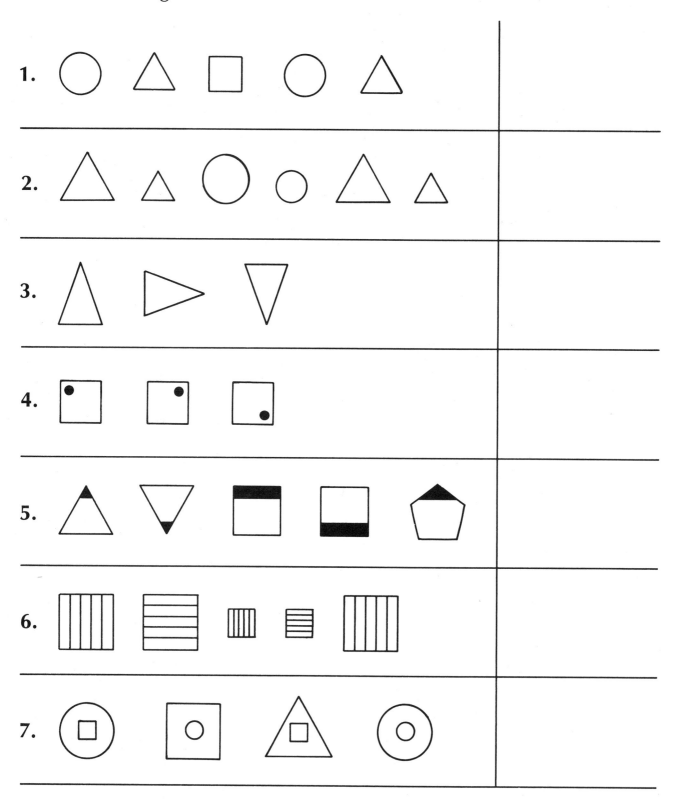

1. ◯ △ ☐ ◯ △

2. △ △ ◯ ◯ △ △

3. △ ▷ ▽

4. ☐ ☐ ☐

5. △ ▽ ☐ ☐ ⬠

6. ▦ ▤ ▥ ▤ ▦

7. ⊡ ⊡ △ ◉

Draw the two figures that come next.

1.

2.

3.

4.

5.

6.

UNIT 4　Number Patterns

Study the pattern rule. Print the missing numbers.

1.　[9] +3 [　] +3 [　] +3 [　] +3 [　] +3 [　]

2.　[2] +4 [　] +4 [　] +4 [　] +4 [　] +4 [　]

3.　[1] +2 [　] +3 [　] +4 [　] +5 [　] +6 [　]

4.　[21] +7 [　] −2 [　] +7 [　] −2 [　] +7 [　]

5.　[34] +1 [　] +2 [　] +1 [　] +2 [　] +1 [　]

6.　[78] −5 [　] +10 [　] −5 [　] +10 [　] −5 [　]

7.　[20] +1 [　] −2 [　] +3 [　] −4 [　] +5 [　]

8.　[10] +0 [　] +10 [　] +20 [　] +30 [　] +40 [　]

Study the pattern. What is the rule?

2	5	8	11			

The rule is: Add 3.

Print the missing numbers in the pattern. What is the rule?

1.

5	10	15				

The rule is: _____

2.

11	22			55		

The rule is: _____

3.

67	56	45				

The rule is: _____

4.

14	9	15	10	16			

The rule is: _____

5.

41	38	35				23	

The rule is: _____

6.

60	68	63	71				

The rule is: _____

Print the numbers that are missing in each pattern.

1. | 86 | 92 | 98 | | | | | |
   |---|---|---|---|---|---|---|---|

2. | 100 | 104 | | 112 | | | | |
   |---|---|---|---|---|---|---|---|

3. | 71 | 61 | | 41 | | | 11 | |
   |---|---|---|---|---|---|---|---|

4. | 16 | 24 | | | 48 | | | |
   |---|---|---|---|---|---|---|---|

5. | 100 | 91 | 83 | 76 | | | | 58 |
   |---|---|---|---|---|---|---|---|

6. | 24 | 26 | 25 | 27 | 26 | | | |
   |---|---|---|---|---|---|---|---|

7. | 5 | 10 | 20 | 25 | | | | 55 |
   |---|---|---|---|---|---|---|---|

8. | 60 | 61 | 64 | 65 | | | | |
   |---|---|---|---|---|---|---|---|

9. | 95 | 90 | 92 | 87 | | | | 81 |
   |---|---|---|---|---|---|---|---|

10. | 52 | 53 | 51 | 54 | | 55 | 49 | |
    |---|---|---|---|---|---|---|---|

Print the number pattern that helps you.
Print each answer in a sentence.

1. Jason is counting the shoes
   in the coatroom.
   How many shoes are there altogether?

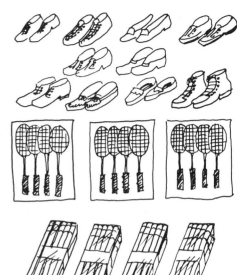

2. Gina is counting the badminton rackets.
   There are 4 rackets in each set.
   How many rackets are there in all?

3. Leslie is counting the new pencils.
   There are 10 pencils in each package.
   How many pencils are there in all?

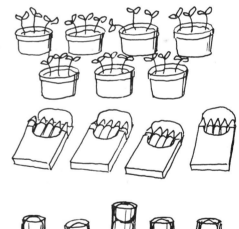

4. Julie is counting pennies.
   She put them in piles of 5.
   How many pennies does Julie have?

5. Jennifer put 3 plants in each pot.
   How many plants are there in all?

6. Each box of crayons has 5 crayons in it.
   How many crayons are there in all?

7. Tennis balls come in packages of 3.
   How many balls are there altogether?

8. Chris is counting paintbrushes.
   There are 6 brushes in each jar.
   How many brushes are there in all?

UNIT 5   Choosing the Example

Print the missing numbers. Choose **+** or **−** .

1. Bobby has 15 🎵 .
   He bought 3 more 🎵 .
   How many 🎵 does he have in all?

   ____
   ____ ===
   ____ in all

2. Mark has 47 🪙 .
   Jan has 59 🪙 .
   How many more 🪙 does Jan have?

   ____ ¢
   ____ ¢ ===
   ____ ¢ more

3. Farrah had 38 ✏ .
   She gave 7 away.
   How many ✏ are left?

   ____
   ____ ===
   ____ are left.

4. 21 🍎 were in a bowl.
   12 🍎 were baked in a pie.
   How many 🍎 are left?

   ____
   ____ ===
   ____ are left.

5. There are 45 🦆 in the pond.
   There are 27 🦢 in the pond.
   How many more 🦆 are in the pond?

   ____
   ____ ===
   ____ more

6. Jack baked 24 🧁 .
   He baked 36 🧁 more.
   How many 🧁 did he bake in all?

   ____
   ____ ===
   ____ in all

Copy the example that matches the problem.
Print each answer in a sentence.

1.	Sara was making a necklace out of beads. She used 53 yellow beads and 38 red beads. How many beads are in the necklace?	53 +38	53 −38
2.	Mary has 160 stamps. Tom has 85 stamps. How many more stamps does Mary have than Tom?	160 − 85	160 + 85
3.	The baker sold 94 orange cupcakes and 87 banana cupcakes. How many cupcakes did the baker sell?	94 −87	94 +87
4.	What is the difference between 82 and 57?	82 +57	82 −57
5.	The pet store had 145 goldfish. 78 of them were female. How many of the goldfish were male?	145 − 78	145 + 78
6.	What is the sum of 89 and 66?	89 +66	89 −66
7.	David has 59¢. Kathy has 76¢. How much more does Kathy have?	76 +59	76 −59
8.	150 planes took off from the airport. 93 planes landed at the airport. How many more planes took off?	150 − 93	150 + 93

Choose the correct example to solve the problems. Print the answers.

Karl has 17 flowers.
Terry has 26 flowers.
  1. How many more flowers does Terry have?
  2. How many flowers are there in all?
	26
	−17
		26
		+17

Linda has 43 pop bottles.
Randy has 25 pop bottles.
  3. How many bottles do they have together?
  4. How many more bottles does Linda have?
	43
	−25
		43
		+25

Jeff drove 56 kilometers.
Oscar drove 45 kilometers.
  5. How many kilometers did they drive in all?
  6. How many more kilometers did Jeff drive?
	56
	−45
		56
		+45

There are 34 books on the first shelf.
There are 19 books on the second shelf.
  7. How many more books on the first shelf?
  8. How many books on both shelves?
	34
	−19
		34
		+19

Anita saved 73¢. Mike saved 87¢. **9.** How much more did Anita save? **10.** How much did they save together?	87 +73	87 −73
Dave has 90 baseball cards. Brenda has 68 baseball cards. **11.** How many baseball cards do they have in all? **12.** How many more baseball cards does Dave have?	90 −68	90 +68

Copy the example that solves the problem. Print the answer.

90	90	90	90
−60	−30	30	+60
		+60	

Dixie and Pat planted a garden. They planted 90 lettuce seeds, 60 cucumber seeds, and 30 radish seeds.

1. How many seeds did they plant in all?

2. How many more lettuce seeds than radish seeds did they plant?

3. How many more lettuce seeds than cucumber seeds did they plant?

4. How many lettuce and cucumber seeds did they plant?

105	58	105	58
−58	+27	−27	−27

105 people went to the ball game. Fifty-eight of them bought just a hot dog. Twenty-seven bought just a drink. The rest bought nothing.

5. How many more bought a hot dog than a drink?

6. How many people bought a hot dog or a drink?

7. How many people did not buy a drink?

8. How many people did not buy a hot dog?

UNIT 6 Using Tables

A table gives a lot of information in an orderly way.

Allowance Received by the Students in Jan's Class

Allowance	Number of Students
25¢	2
40¢	6
50¢	8
75¢	7
$1.00	3

How many students get more than 45¢ a week?

Use the numbers in the table to solve the problem.

8   students get 50¢.
7   students get 75¢.
+3   students get $1.00.
18   students get more than 45¢ for allowance.

Use numbers from the table above to solve the problems.

1. How many students get 40¢?

2. How many more students get 75¢ than 25¢ for allowance?

3. How many students get 40¢ or 50¢ for allowance?

**Boys and Girls in each Grade
at Kingsley School**

Grades	Girls	Boys
Grade 1	11	13
Grade 2	14	14
Grade 3	15	16
Grade 4	12	17
Grade 5	11	18
Grade 6	16	15
Grade 7	17	16

Use the numbers in the table to solve the problems.

1. How many girls and boys altogether in Grade 3?

2. Are there more boys in Grade 4 or Grade 5?

3. How many more girls in Grade 7 than in Grade 1?

4. How many boys and girls in all in Grade 2?

5. Are there more boys in Grade 7 or girls in Grade 6?

6. How many boys and girls are there in Grade 4 and Grade 5?

7. How many girls are there in Kingsley School?

8. How many girls and boys in all are there in Kingsley School?

Put the information into a table. Answer the questions.

The students in two classes baked cookies for a bake sale. Mrs. Sellinger's class baked 60 chocolate chip cookies and 82 peanut butter cookies. Mr. Wood's class baked 36 chocolate chip cookies and 76 peanut butter cookies.

1. **Cookies Made for the Bake Sale**

Cookies	Mrs. Sellinger's Class	Mr. Wood's Class
Chocolate chip		
Peanut butter		

2. How many cookies did Mr. Wood's class bake in all?

3. How many chocolate chip cookies were made in all?

4. Which class made more cookies?

5. How many more peanut butter cookies were made by Mrs. Sellinger's class than by Mr. Wood's class?

6. How many more peanut butter cookies than chocolate chip cookies did Mr. Wood's class make?

7. How many more chocolate chip cookies were made by Mrs. Sellinger's class than by Mr. Wood's class?

8. How many cookies were made for the bake sale altogether?

Put the information into a table. Answer the questions.

On Wednesday, 39 adults and 52 children went to the Mayfair Zoo. On Thursday, 32 children and 15 adults went to the Mayfair Zoo. On Friday, 47 adults and 27 children went to the Mayfair Zoo. On Saturday, 63 children and 40 adults went to the Mayfair Zoo.

1.

People Who Attended the Zoo

People	Wednesday	Thursday	Friday	Saturday
Adults				
Children				

2. How many people went to the zoo on Friday?

3. Did more children or adults go to the zoo on Saturday?

4. How many children went to the zoo on Wednesday and on Thursday?

5. How many children went to the zoo altogether?

6. How many adults went to the zoo altogether?

7. How many more children went to the zoo on Wednesday than on Friday?

8. How many people went to the zoo in all?

UNIT 7 Review Problems

1. You want to take a shower.
Which does *not* belong?

a.  **b.**  **c.**  **d.**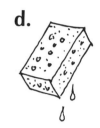

2. This lamp will not light.
Which do you need to make it light?

a.   **b.** 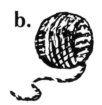 **c.**   **d.**

3. Your nails are too long.
Which do you need to make them shorter?

a.  **b.** 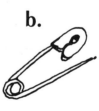 **c.**  **d.**

4. You are making a sandwich.
Which does not belong?

a. **b.** 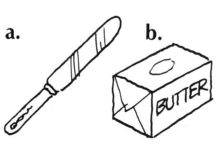 **c.** **d.**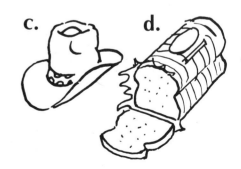

Put the pictures in order. Answer the questions.

1.

A   B   C

D   E   F

2. Which comes first?

3. Which comes fourth?

4. When does picture F come in the story?

Read the story. Answer the questions.

The Bakery

Early one morning, Mr. Albert made many things to sell in his bakery. He made 25 loaves of white bread and 18 loaves of rye bread. He made 56 chocolate chip cookies, 64 sugar cookies, and 48 peanut butter cookies. He also made 10 chocolate cakes.

5. How many more loaves of white bread than rye bread did he make?

6. How many cookies did he make in all?

7. Mr. Albert sold all but one chocolate cake. How many chocolate cakes did he sell?

Draw the two figures that come next in each pattern.

1.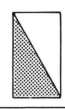

2.

3.

Print the numbers that are missing in each pattern.

4.

132	129	126			117		111

5.

60	70	65	75	70			

6.

3	4	6	9	13			

Print the number pattern. Answer the question in a sentence.

7. There are 3 rows with 8 chocolates in each row. How many chocolates are in the box?

8. Rod is counting his nickels. How much money does he have?

9. There are 4 wheels on each car. How many wheels are there altogether?

Choose the correct example to solve each problem. Answer the questions.

a.	91		**b.**	91		**c.**	65
	−83			−65			+91

Tina, Sharon, and Steve went bowling. Tina scored 65. Sharon scored 91. Steve scored 83.

1. How much more did Sharon score than Steve?

2. How much did Tina and Sharon score together?

3. How much more did Steve score than Tina?

_____

Use the numbers in the table to solve the problems.

Favorite Pies of Students in Three Classes

Favorite Pie	Jean's Class	Lucy's Class	Jason's Class
Apple	14	16	16
Cherry	17	12	15

4. How many children are there in Jean's class?

5. How many more children in Lucy's class like apple pie than cherry pie?

6. Which pie do the children in Jason's class like better?

7. How many more children in Lucy's class than in Jean's class like apple pie?

UNIT 8   Using Pictures

Sometimes a picture can help you solve a problem.

Problem:

    Raul had 9 tennis balls.

    He gave 5 away.

    How many tennis balls does he have left?

Solution:

The picture shows that Raul has 4 tennis balls left.

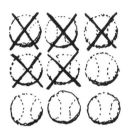

Write the letter for the picture that matches the problem.

1.   Sandy had 5 dimes and 3 nickels.
    She spent 3 dimes and 1 nickel.
    What coins does she have left?

a.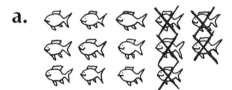

2.   Nadia caught 14 fish.
    She threw 5 back into the water.
    How many fish does Nadia have left?

b.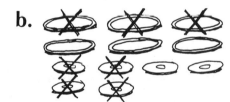

3.   Mike had 5 plates and 8 saucers to wash.
    He washed 4 plates and 2 saucers.
    What dishes does he have left to wash?

c.

4.   Leona had 6 plates and 6 saucers to dry.
    She dried 3 plates and 4 saucers.
    What dishes does she have left to dry?

d.

5.   Alex caught 11 fish.
    He gave 4 away.
    How many does he have now?

e.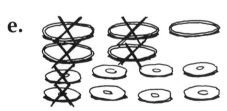

Copy the picture.
Use it to help answer the question.

1. Sally had 12 raffle tickets to sell.
   Her mom bought 4.
   Her dad bought 3.
   How many tickets did she have left?

2. There are 16 plants at Kate's house.
   6 are in the kitchen.
   3 are in the bedroom.
   How many plants are in the rest of the house?

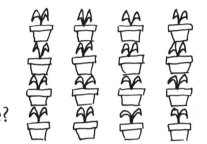

3. Chuck had 20 cookies.
   He ate 5 cookies.
   He gave 5 cookies to Sonja.
   He gave 3 cookies to Glen.
   How many cookies did he have left?

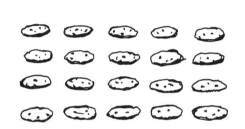

4. Martha made 13 cups of coffee.
   She drank 2 cups herself.
   Doreen drank 4 cups.
   Sheila drank 3 cups.
   How many cups of coffee were left?

5. Mario had 4 nickels, 2 dimes, and 3 quarters.
   He spent 1 quarter, 1 dime, and 2 nickels.
   What coins does he have left?

6. There were 3 hammers and 10 nails in the garage.
   Christie took 1 hammer and 3 nails.
   What tools were left in the garage?

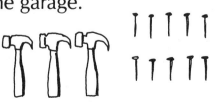

Problem:

A bicycle has 2 wheels.
There are 5 bicycles.
How many wheels are there?

Solution:

        $5 \times 2 = 10$

There are 10 wheels.

Draw a picture to help answer each question.
Print a number sentence to go with each picture.

1. There are 6 triangles.
    How many sides are there?

2. There are 4 squares.
    How many sides are there?

3. A box of crayons has 8 crayons in it.
    There are 3 boxes.
    How many crayons are there?

4. Evelyn's kitchen floor is made of tiles.
    There were 9 rows and 8 tiles in each row.
    How many tiles are there?

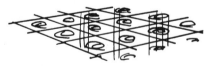

5. There are 3 posters.
    Each poster has 6 flags on it.
    Each flag has 2 stripes.
    How many stripes altogether?

Draw a picture to help answer each question.
Print your answer.

1. Dennis has 11 marbles.
   He trades 2 red marbles for 4 blue marbles.
   How many marbles does he have now?

2. Frances has 9 cookies.
   She trades 3 coconut cookies for 5 lemon cookies.
   How many cookies does she have now?

3. Terri made a triangle out of matches.
   Each side was 14 matches long.
   What is the perimeter of the triangle?

4. A playground is in the shape of a square.
   Each side is 15 meters long.
   Trees grow every 3 meters around the rim of the playground.
   How many trees are there?

5. There were 18 pickets in a fence.
   Every third picket was yellow.
   How many pickets were yellow?

6. Della started practicing piano at 3:50.
   She finished at 4:20.
   For how long did Della practice piano?

7. Jorma's ball game started at 6:10.
   It ended at 8:00.
   How long did the ball game last?

UNIT 9 Guessing and Testing

> Sometimes the easiest way to solve a problem is to guess an answer and test to see if it is correct. If it is *not* correct, a better guess is made.

1. Find two numbers whose sum is 20 and whose difference is 8.

2. Find two numbers whose sum is 35 and whose difference is 13.

3. Find two numbers whose sum is 63 and whose difference is 29.

4. Find two numbers whose sum is 88 and whose difference is 34.

Read the problems. Each letter stands for a digit.
Find the missing digits.

5.
```
  B6A
 +3B3
 ----
  587
```
A = _
B = _

6.
```
  B4A
 +1A5
 ----
  A44
```
A = _
B = _

7.
```
  A43
 +2A7
 ----
  8BB
```
A = _
B = _

8.
```
  9B6
 -16A
 ----
  B2A
```
A = _
B = _

9.
```
  7BA
 -B46
 ----
  479
```
A = _
B = _

10.
```
  8A6
 -A5B
 ----
  4B9
```
A = _
B = _

Guess and test to find the correct solutions.

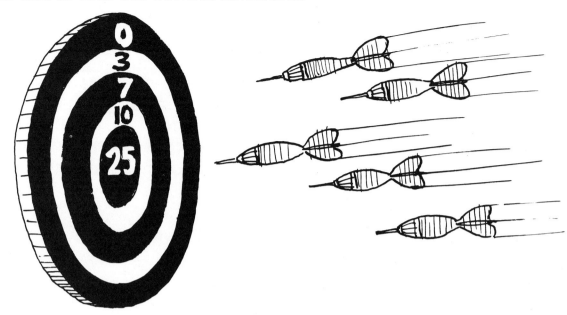

1. How could you score 45 points with 5 darts?

2. How could you score 30 points?

3. Find another way to score 30 points.

4. How could you score 52 points?

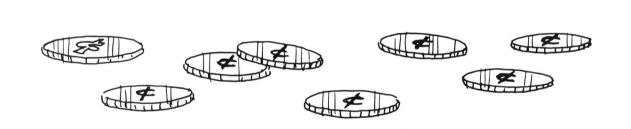

5. Mary has eight coins that have a total sum of 47¢.
   What coins does Mary have?

Each of these things has wheels.

1. How many bicycles and cars would you need to get 10 wheels?

2. How many unicycles and cars would you need to get 13 wheels?

3. How would you get 23 wheels?

4. How would you get 16 wheels?

Each of these figures has corners.

5. How many squares would you need to get 16 corners?

6. How many squares and triangles would you need to get 17 corners?

7. How many triangles would you need to get 15 corners?

8. How many triangles and rectangles would you need to get 25 corners?

Doug wanted to buy some things to add to his lunch.
He had $1.00 to spend.

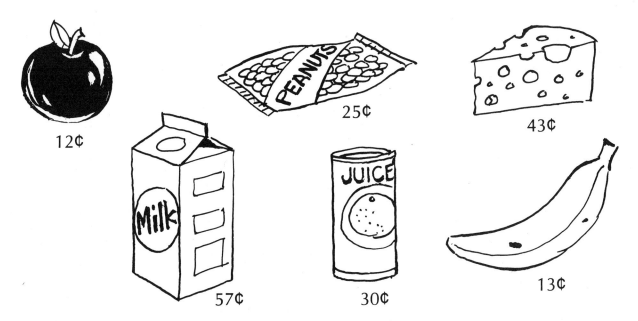

12¢

25¢

43¢

57¢

30¢

13¢

1. Which two items could Doug buy that would cost exactly $1.00?

2. If he buys milk, how many bananas could he buy?

3. How many bags of peanuts could Doug buy?

4. If Doug buys two pieces of cheese, what else could he buy?

5. What is the largest number of apples Doug could buy for $1.00?

6. What can Doug buy so he gets 18¢ change?

7. What can Doug buy so he gets 7¢ change?

8. If Doug buys juice and cheese, what one thing would he not be able to buy?

9. How would you spend $1.00?

UNIT 10   Two Steps

Sometimes it takes more than one step to solve a problem.

Problem:

Mom baked 16 cookies.
Cheryl ate 4 cookies.
Randy ate 6 cookies.
How many cookies are left?

Solution:

Step 1

First find out how many cookies were eaten altogether.   4
Add 4 cookies and 6 cookies.   +6

10 cookies were eaten altogether.   10

Step 2

Then find out how many cookies are left.   16
Subtract 10 from 16 cookies.   −10

6 cookies are left.   6

Use two steps to solve these problems.
Show your work.

1. 18 people were on the bus.
     4 people got off.
     7 people got on.
    How many people are on the bus now?

2. Dale had 19 pieces of wool.
    She used 8 for shoelaces.
    She used 6 for hair ribbons.
    How many pieces of wool does Dale have left?

3. Mr. Rossi caught 12 salmon.
   He caught 13 trout.
   He threw 5 fish back in the water.
   How many fish does he have now?

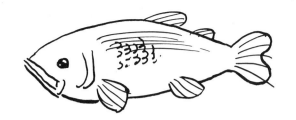

4. Art had 20 cups to wash.
   He washed 8.
   His sister gave him 5 more to wash.
   How many cups does he have to wash now?

5. Tim had 84 stamps.
   41 were from Germany and 23 were from France.
   How many stamps were not from Germany or France?

6. Tika had 65¢.
   He spent 33¢.
   He earned another 25¢.
   How much does Tika have now?

7. Jeff played tennis with Bob for 25 minutes.
   Then he played with Wendy for 25 minutes.
   How much longer would Jeff need to play
   if he wanted to play for an hour?

8. Samba bought 45 cm of blue material.
   She bought 30 cm of red material.
   If she wanted 1 m of material
   altogether, how much more does she need?

Use two steps to solve these problems.
Show your work.

1. Adelaide had 40 names in her address book.
   She crossed out 12 names.
   She added 8 new names.
   How many names are in Adelaide's address book now?

2. Liz had to put stamps on 113 envelopes.
   She put stamps on 54 envelopes.
   Then her mother gave her 37 more envelopes which needed stamps.
   How many envelopes does she have to put stamps on now?

3. Saul had 146 boxes of mints to sell.
   He sold 49 boxes on Friday and 36 boxes on Saturday.
   How many boxes does he have left to sell?

4. 153 tickets were sold for the school concert.
   65 tickets were for Tuesday night.
   27 tickets were for Wednesday night.
   The rest were for Thursday night.
   How many tickets were sold for Thursday night?

5. An elephant can eat 1400 pounds of food a day.
   For breakfast he ate 640 pounds of food.
   For lunch he ate 488 pounds of food.
   How many pounds of food can he have for dinner?

6. 425 boys and 357 girls entered the puzzle contest.
   900 children are allowed to enter.
   How many more children can still enter the contest?

Solve the problems.

1. Oranges were on sale 5 for 45¢.
   Apples cost 12¢ each.
   How much for one apple and one orange?

2. A toy ball cost 9¢.
   A bat costs three times as much as a ball.
   How much do two bats cost?

3. Omar had 27 stickers.
   He gave 3 friends 8 stickers each.
   How many does he have left?

4. Rae had 18 toy whistles.
   He gave 6 friends 2 whistles each.
   How many does he have left?

5. Jerry saved 5¢.
   Hans saved three times as much.
   How much did they save altogether?

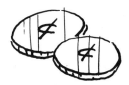

6. Lena saved 9¢.
   Randy saved twice as much.
   How much did they save altogether?

7. Greg saved 8¢.
   Risa saved three times as much.
   How much more did Risa save than Greg?

UNIT 11 Too Much Information

Some problems tell more than you need to know.

Problem:

How many rectangles?

Solution:

There are 6 rectangles.

1. How many squares?

2. How many triangles?

3. How many circles?

4. How many triangles?

5. How many rectangles?

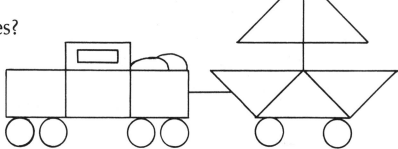

Write the letters for the facts you do not need.

1. **a.** 36 ☕   **c.** 36 🥏

    b. 18  🥄   **d.** 72 🥛

    How many cups and glasses?

2. **a.** 45 🧦   **c.** 31 👠

    b. 56  👞   **d.** 39 🧤

    How many shoes?

3. **a.** 129 ⭘   **c.** 97 🧶

    b. 168  🎀   **d.** 85 🪡

    How many more bows than buttons?

4. **a.** 233 🍬   **c.** 369 🍭

    b. 300  🍫   **d.** 400 🪣

    How many suckers?

5. **a.** 750 △   **c.** 955 ◯

    b. 923 ☐   **d.** 795 ▭

    How many more squares than triangles?

Write the letters for the facts you do *not* need.
Solve the problems.

1. **a.** The red paper is 56 inches long.

 b. The yellow paper is 38 inches long.

 c. The orange paper is 43 inches long.

 d. The red paper is 20 inches wide.

 How long are the red and orange papers together?

2. **a.** 375 children go to McBride School.

 b. 21 teachers are at Jaspar School.

 c. 403 children go to Sunrise School.

 d. 421 children go to Jaspar School.

 How many more children go to Jaspar School than McBride School?

3. **a.** Jerry drove 373 miles on Friday.

 b. He drove 589 miles on Saturday.

 c. He drove 142 miles on Sunday.

 d. Frank drove 262 miles on Friday.

 How far did Jerry drive on Friday and Saturday?

4. **a.** At the pet store, there were 5 cages of baby snakes.

 b. There were 3 cages of big snakes.

 c. There were 4 cages of baby rabbits.

 d. There were 9 baby snakes in each cage.

 How many baby snakes were there at the pet store?

5. **a.** Lisa drew 6 rows of leaves.

 b. There were 6 leaves in each row.

 c. 17 of the leaves were red.

 d. 11 of the leaves were green.

 How many leaves did Lisa draw altogether?

Solve the problems.

1. Maria had $5.31.
   Henry had $3.89.
   Maria spent $2.07.
   How much does Maria have left?

2. Stephanie played baseball for 45 minutes.
   She rested for 20 minutes.
   She played soccer for 35 minutes.
   How long did Stephanie play games?

3. Harley caught 59 tuna.
   Scott caught 70 trout.
   Katie caught 63 salmon.
   How many more fish did Scott catch than Katie?

4. Mrs. Dow is 52 years old.
   Mrs. Marden is 45 years old.
   Mr. Smith is 61 years old.
   How much older is Mr. Smith than Mrs. Dow?

5. In an orchard, there were 128 cherry trees.
   There were 162 pine trees.
   There were 236 apple trees.
   How many fruit trees were there in the orchard?

6. 500 people came to a picnic.
   281 people came by bike.
   176 people came by cars.
   The rest of the people walked.
   How many people rode to the picnic?

UNIT 12   More Than One Question

> **Sometimes a problem has more than one question.**
> **To solve the problem, answer one question at a time.**

Use the pictograph for the facts you need.

Cory, Bruce, and Kella built a fort.

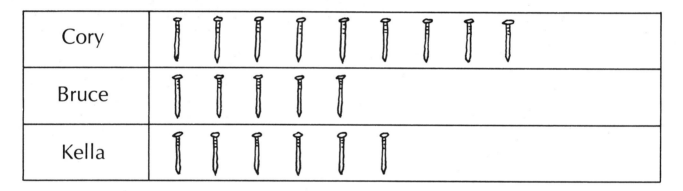 stands for 5 nails.

Cory	🔩 🔩 🔩 🔩 🔩 🔩 🔩 🔩 🔩
Bruce	🔩 🔩 🔩 🔩 🔩
Kella	🔩 🔩 🔩 🔩 🔩 🔩

1. How many nails did Cory use?

2. How many nails did Bruce use?

3. How many nails did Kella use?

4. How many more nails did Cory use than Kella?

5. How many nails did Bruce and Kella use together?

6. Who used the most nails?

7. How many nails were used altogether to build the fort?

Use the pictograph for the facts you need.

The children had a book club during the summer.

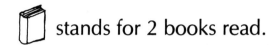 stands for 2 books read.

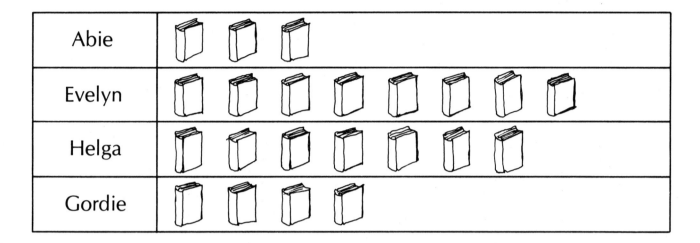

1. Who read the most books?

2. How many books did Abie read?

3. How many books did Helga and Gordie read together?

4. How many more books did Evelyn read than Abie?

5. How many books did Evelyn and Helga read together?

6. How many books did the children read altogether?

7. How many more books did Evelyn and Gordie read than Helga and Abie?

UNIT 13   Missing Information

Some problems do not give all the facts you need to find the answer.

Problem:

5 packages of golf balls.
How many golf balls in all?

Solution:

You can solve the problem if you know that there are 3 golf balls in each package.

$$5 \times 3 = 15$$

There are 15 golf balls in all.

Write the letter for the picture you need.
Solve each problem.

1. 40 golf tees in all.
How many golf tees in each bag?

2. 9 golf clubs in each bag.
How many golf clubs in all?

3. 15 tennis balls in all.
How many tennis balls in each can?

4. 6 ping pong balls in each package.
How many ping pong balls in all?

5. 36 ping pong paddles in all.
How many ping pong paddles in each set?

a.

b.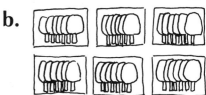

c.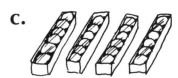

d.

e.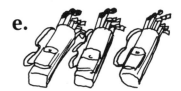

Write the fact that you need for each problem.
Use the pictures to help you.

1. Debbie and B.J. bought 3 packages of light bulbs.
   There are _____ bulbs in each package.
   How many light bulbs did they buy in all?

2. They bought 2 packages of tape.
   There are _____ in each package.
   How many rolls of tape did they buy in all?

3. They bought 42 screws.
   There are _____ in each package.
   How many packages of screws did they buy?

4. They bought 4 packages of nails.
   There are _____ in each package.
   How many nails did they buy?

5. They bought 24 plugs.
   There are _____ in each package.
   How many packages of plugs did they buy in all?

6. They bought 18 balls of string.
   There are _____ in each package.
   How many packages of string did they buy?

Write the letter for the fact you need.
Solve each problem.

1. Liz had 10 marbles.
   How many marbles were red?

   a. $\frac{5}{10}$ of the marbles were red.
   b. She played marbles for 10 minutes.

2. Gail had 5 records.
   How many records are broken?

   a. Sal has 3 records.   b. $\frac{2}{5}$ of the records are broken.

3. There were 8 flowers in the vase.
   How many of the flowers were tulips?

   a. $\frac{2}{8}$ of the flowers are tulips.   b. $\frac{4}{8}$ of the flowers are daisies.

4. Max wrote 6 letters.
   How many did he send airmail?

   a. He sent $\frac{3}{6}$ of them airmail.
   b. $\frac{2}{6}$ of them were on postcards.

5. Olga had 10 pieces of chocolate.
   She ate $\frac{2}{10}$ of the pieces.
   Who ate more?

   a. The pieces were square.   b. Sylvia ate $\frac{6}{10}$ of the pieces.

6. Myra had a ribbon 10 cm long.
   How long is the ribbon that is left?

   a. She had another ribbon 13 cm long.
   b. She cut off $\frac{3}{10}$ of the ribbon.

Solve each problem.
Use the chart for the facts you need.

Animals at the Zoo	
Monkeys	8 in each cage
Bears	4 in each cage
Ducks	6 in each pond
Squirrels	5 in each tree
Snakes	7 in each cage
Parrots	3 in each cage
Giraffes	2 in each cage

1. Stan counted the bears in 4 cages.
   How many bears did he count in all?

2. Ivan could only see $\frac{1}{2}$ of the ducks in one pond.
   How many ducks could Ivan see?

3. There were 28 snakes at the zoo.
   How many cages had snakes in them?

4. Darcy counted 12 parrots.
   How many cages of parrots did he count?

5. Jennifer counted the squirrels in 5 trees.
   How many squirrels did she count altogether?

6. One half of the monkeys in one cage were swinging
   by their tails.
   How many monkeys were swinging by their tails?

UNIT 14   Reasonable Answers

When you solve a problem, ask yourself if your answer makes sense.

Problem:

Sarbi had $8.19.
She spent $3.11.
About how much does she have left?

a. About $11.00   **b.** About $5.00.

Solution:

Does about $11.00 make sense?
No, $11.00 is more than Sarbi had at first.

Does about $5.00 make sense?
Let's estimate the answer.

| $8.19 is about $8.00 | $8.00 |
| $3.11 is about $3.00 | −$3.00 |

Subtract to find out how much $5.00
Sarbi has left.

The answer should be about $5.00.

Write the letter of the answer that makes sense.
Tell why the other answer does not make sense.

1. Rick ran 12 km on Tuesday.
    He ran 9 km on Wednesday.
    About how far did he run on both days?

    a. About 3 km   **b.** About 20 km

2. There are 32 students in Shayne's class.
There are 29 students in Philip's class.
About how many students are in both classes?

a. About 30 students   **b.** About 60 students

3. Stella made 55 muffins.
Grace made 36 muffins.
About how many more muffins did Stella make than Grace?

a. About 20 muffins   **b.** About 50 muffins

4. 298 people went to a party.
163 people wore costumes..
About how many people did not wear costumes?

a. About 300 people   **b.** About 140 people

5. James spent $4.95.
Janet spent $9.05.
About how much more did Janet spend?

a. About $4.00   **b.** About $9.00

6. Leslie guessed there were 399 jellybeans in the jar.
Scott guessed there were 350 jellybeans in the jar.
About how many more did Leslie guess than Scott?

a. About 750 jellybeans   **b.** About 50 jellybeans

7. There are 4 decals in a package.
Barbie used 8 packages.
About how many decals did Barbie use?

a. About 30 decals   **b.** About 10 decals

Write the letter of the answer that makes sense.
Tell why the other answer does not make sense.

1. Ralph has $4.25.
    Sandy has $2.80.
    Hank has $2.20.
    About how much do they have in all?

    a. About $7.00   **b.** About $9.00

2. Ron has 2 quarters and 1 dime.
    Alicia has 3 quarters and 3 dimes.
    About how much more does Alicia have?

    a. About 50¢   **b.** About $1.00

3. Chuck's backyard is shaped like a square.
    Each side is 7 m long.
    About how long is it all the way around Chuck's backyard?

    a. About 20 m   **b.** About 30 m

4. It is 23 m from the house to the tree
    and 31 m from the tree to the river.
    About how far is it from the house to the river?

    a. About 30 m   **b.** About 50 m

5. Tracy took 12 minutes to get dressed for school.
    She took 17 minutes to eat breakfast.
    About how long did it take Tracy to do both?

    a. About 30 minutes   **b.** About 20 minutes

6. A radio cost $7.80.
It went on sale for $5.99.
About how much would you save if you
bought the radio on sale?

a. About $13.80   **b.** About $1.80

7. Peaches are 3 for 25¢.
About how much does each peach cost?

a. About 8¢   **b.** About 5¢

8. Toy airplanes are 4 for 21¢.
About how much does each airplane cost?

a. About 9¢   **b.** About 5¢

9. Bobby's books weigh 7.6 pounds.
His shoes weigh 3.2 pounds.
How much do his books and shoes weigh together?

a. About 11 pounds   **b.** About 5 pounds

10. Dad bought 2.2 pounds of potatoes.
He bought 2.0 pounds of tomatoes.
He bought 1.5 pounds of onions.
About how many pounds of vegetables did Dad buy?

a. About 6 pounds   **b.** About 4 pounds

11. Mandy had a rope which was 0.9 feet long.
She tied 1.2 feet of rope to it.
About how much length of rope does she have now?

a. About 0.3 feet   **b.** About 2.0 feet

UNIT 15   Review Problems

Finish these patterns.

1.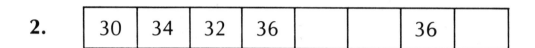

2. | 30 | 34 | 32 | 36 | | | 36 | |

---

3. Wendy is counting the diamonds in the rings.
How many diamonds are there?

Copy the example that solves the problem. Print the answer.

34 children go to the morning kindergarten class.
29 children go to the afternoon kindergarten class.

$$\begin{array}{rr} 34 & 34 \\ -29 & +29 \\ \hline \end{array}$$

4. How many children go to kindergarten in all?

5. How many more children go to the morning
class than the afternoon class?

favorite pets in two grades

Pets	Grade 1	Grade 5
Dogs	35	42
Cats	23	14
Fish	17	28

6. How many children in Grade 1 and Grade 5 chose fish as their favorite pet?

7. How many more children in Grade 1 chose dogs than chose fish?

8. How many more children in Grade 5 chose dogs than chose cats?

---

9. Find a number whose sum is 52 and whose difference is 28.

10. Find a number whose sum is 75 and whose difference is 31.

Write the letter for the fact you need.

11. There were 8 cars in a traffic jam.
How many of the cars were blue?

   a. $\frac{2}{8}$ of them were sportscars.   **b.** $\frac{3}{8}$ of them were blue.

Write the letter of the answer that makes sense.
Tell why the other answer does not make sense.

12. Greg has 29 pencil crayons.
Cal has 53 pencil crayons.
About how many more pencil crayons does Cal have?

   a. About 80 pencil crayons   **b.** About 20 pencil crayons

Draw a picture to help answer the question. Print your answer.

13. There were 24 animals in the parade.
Every third one was a dog.
How many dogs were in the parade?

14. There were 2 puppies in each basket.
There were 3 baskets.
Each puppy has 5 spots.
How many spots in all?

15.

Maria has 6 coins that have a total sum of 81¢.
What coins does Maria have?

55¢   85¢   65¢   45¢

16. Which two items cost exactly $1.00?

17. Which two items cost exactly $1.50?

18. What can you buy so you get 60¢ change from $2.00?

---

19. Brad had 50 boxes of cookies to sell.
He sold 12 boxes on Monday and 23 boxes on Tuesday.
How many boxes does he have left to sell?

---

20. Estelle had $8.65.
She spent $2.70.
She earned $4.15.
How much does she have now?

21. There were 226 people on the beach.
87 people were swimming.
103 people were suntanning.
How many more people were suntanning than swimming?

Ruby, Bryan, and Jorge collected bottle caps.

stands for 10 bottle caps.

Ruby	(4 caps)
Bryan	(7 caps)
Jorge	(5 caps)

22. How many bottle caps did Bryan collect?

23. How many more bottle caps did Bryan collect than Ruby?

24. How many more bottle caps did Ruby and Jorge collect than Bryan?

25. Maureen used 2 boxes of pipe cleaners.
How many pipe cleaners did she use?

Pipe Cleaners
4 in each box

26. Elana made flowers using 15 petals.
How many bags of petals did she use?

Flower Petals
5 in each bag

27. The clown sold 241 bags of peanuts at the circus.
She sold 139 bags of popcorn.
About how many bags of peanuts and popcorn did the clown sell?

a. About 380 bags   **b.** About 250 bags

Teacher's Resources

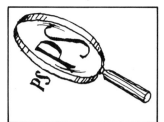

Problem Solving

What is it?

Definitions of mathematical problem solving and descriptions of its scope continue to be developed by teachers and researchers. George Polya has said that to solve a problem is to find a way where no way is known offhand, to find a way out of difficulty, to find a way around an obstacle, to attain a desired end that is not immediately attainable by appropriate means.

A supermarket manager wants to build a square pyramid with cans of apple juice. The bottom layer is to be 8 cans wide.
How many cans will the display use?

Its Importance

Achieving success in problem solving continues to be an important student objective for teachers at all grade levels. Recent mathematics assessments have highlighted the fact that while most students do well on computational items, they perform poorly on exercises requiring problem solving or application of mathematical skills.

The National Council of Teachers of Mathematics Priorities in School Mathematics Project (PRISM) found that classroom teachers, mathematics educators, and lay people all supported the position that problem solving should receive greater emphasis in the curriculum. In their recommendation for school mathematics in the 1980's, the N.C.T.M. proposed that problem solving be the focus of school mathematics.

As a result of these concerns, mathematics educators across the United States have made problem solving a major focal point.

Where do we start?

By its very nature, problem solving is frustrating. Since answers do not come quickly, it is easy to become impatient and avoid future problem situations. Consequently, it is crucial that a positive, low pressure, relaxed classroom atmosphere be used so that student interest in and success with problem solving can be attained.

The following suggestions can help to create a pleasant problem-solving atmosphere in the classroom.

1. Let the students feel successful.
2. Start with easy problems.
3. Work in small groups.
4. Relax the usual success-and-failure standards.
5. Be patient.
6. Remove pressures.
7. Have fun.
8. Be positive.
9. Share ideas and strategies.

What does it involve?

Heuristics, such as George Polya's four-step problem solving procedure, form a conceptual framework for productive problem solving. Polya's procedure is well known and respected by curriculum developers, teachers, and students.

> **Polya's Plan**
> 1. Understand the problem.
> 2. Devise a plan.
> 3. Carry out the plan.
> 4. Look back.

The program closely follows Polya's four-step procedure with its *IDEA* plan.

> 1. **I**dentify.
> 2. **D**ecide.
> 3. **E**valuate.
> 4. **A**nswer.

IDENTIFY

The first step for successful problem solving is to identify all pertinent facts.

1. What are the facts?
2. Are important *facts missing*?
3. Are *too many facts* given?
4. Can the facts be *restated* more simply?
5. What are the *key words* in the problem?

Once the important facts of a problem are noted, the second step is to decide on a plan for its solution.

1. **Guess and test.**
   Can you guess a solution? Does it solve the problem or lead to a dead end? What did you learn from your guess?
2. **Use charts, tables, or graphs.**
   Can you collect and organize the facts in a table or chart? Does a bar, line, or circle graph highlight important facts?
3. **Use patterns.**
   Is there a possible pattern?
4. **Choose the operation.**
   Can the problem be solved by adding, subtracting, multiplying, or dividing? Are several arithmetic steps involved?
5. **Use diagrams and pictures.**
   Will a sketch of the situation help you decide on the solution plan?
6. **Use a simpler problem.**
   Will a similar but simpler problem point out a solution plan?
7. **Act it out.**

EVALUATE

After the plan for solving the problem has been decided, it is carried out.

1. Use a number sentence.
2. Use a diagram, picture, or model.

Once a solution to a problem has been found, it is essential that one looks back at the answer.

1. Estimate the answer. Is the solution found *reasonable*?
2. Is there another, and possibly shorter, way to solve the problem?
3. Explain your solution.
4. Look for different solutions.

Teaching Suggestions

1. Allow time for group discussion. Talk about the facts presented. See that the students *understand* the problem. Share student ideas and *strategies* for solving the problem.

2. Encourage students to work in pairs. Motivation is greatly increased when students can share ideas. Students can learn from each other.

3. Do not assign work as you would from the basic textbook. *Challenge* the students to do a certain number of problems and then allow them to do a few problems of their own choice. Stress quality rather than quantity.

4. Encourage flexibility. Accept different problem-solving strategies. Share different solutions.

5. Change standards for the appearance of student work. The student work will not usually look like a textbook assignment. Do not always require number sentences to be written for the answer. Encourage pictures and diagrams. Students should be able to write *concluding statements* to the problems.

6. Have the students keep a problem-solving notebook. Similar problems which have previously been solved can then be referred to.

7. Provide appropriate *hints* without giving away the answer. Remind the students of the various problem-solving strategies. Pictures or diagrams can often be a hint to a problem's solution.

8. Simplify problems, as needed. Sometimes a problem is overwhelmingly complex and it is better to start with a simpler problem.

9. Extend problems, creating variations to similar, previously-solved problems. For example, once the following problem is solved, try the given variations.

> If 5 children trade one baseball card with each other child, how many different trades would take place?

VARIATIONS

(1) Change the number of children.
(2) Change the number of cards traded.
(3) Change the *given* and *wanted* information. (Give the number of trades. Ask for the number of children.)

10. Create a problem-solving center, puzzle of the day, and bulletin board. Maintain a learning environment rich in manipulatives and ancillary supplies ready for use in problem solving.

Unit 1: Sorting and Classifying
Objective

Organize information by sorting and classifying.

Notes

The exercises in this unit are preliminary exercises for deciding which facts are necessary for solving a problem.

On the first two pages, students are asked to sort items according to physical attributes, geometric properties, and function, and according to being a "part of" (e.g. part of a bicycle).

On page 2, students are asked to write the letter of the item that does *not* belong in each set. On page 3, they are asked to write the letter of the item that does belong in each set.

The exercises on pages 4 and 5 require students to classify items according to their function. On page 4, students are asked to write the letter of the item that fits the purpose of the problem. On page 5, they are asked to write the letter of the item that does *not* fit the purpose of the problem.

Unit 2: Reading Stories
Objectives

Decide the correct sequence for picture stories.
Choose the correct pictures to represent stories.
Answer questions after reading a story.

Notes

The first two pages of this unit provide experiences in ordering. For each series of lettered pictures, students are to place those letters in the correct order according to the pictures. They also answer questions about that sequence using ordinal numbers.

On page 8, students write the letter of the picture that matches the story. The direction of the arrow indicates addition or subtraction and the numbers are represented within the pictures.

Students are asked to read the story on page 9 and answer the related questions.

Unit 3: Geometry Patterns
Objective

Detect and continue pictorial and positional patterns.

Notes

The exercises on the two pages of this unit require students to detect a pictorial pattern, a positional pattern, or a combination of both, and to supply the next two figures in each pattern. Some patterns employ two attributes in different sequences.

Unit 4: Number Patterns
Objectives
Detect and continue number patterns.
Use number patterns to help solve word problems.

Notes

On the first page of this unit, pattern rules are given for each exercise. The student is to fill in the missing numbers.

On page 13, the student is to supply the missing numbers and state the rule for each pattern.

On page 14, the student is to supply the missing numbers in each pattern. The rule for the patterns are limited to addition, subtraction, or a combination of both.

The student is to use number patterns to help solve the word problems on page 15.

Unit 5: Choosing the Example
Objective

Choose the operation needed to solve a word problem after reading it and focus on the key words that help to indicate the operation required.

Notes

The exercises in this unit provide experiences for the student to decide the correct operation to solve given word problems. Stress the reading and digesting of the entire word problem before focusing on the key words.

On the first page, students are to choose the operation as well as supply the numbers to form a suitable equation for each word problem.

On the following three pages, students are to copy the example that solves each problem and complete the solution.

Unit 6: Using Tables
Objectives

Read and construct simple tables.
Solve problems using information from tables.

Notes

It is important that students not only be able to read tables but also construct them.

The first two pages of this unit present complete tables. Students are to read and interpret the tables using the given information to answer the questions.

The last two pages present information and blank tables. Students are to place the information into the tables and then answer the questions.

Unit 7: Review
Objective

Review the following problem solving strategies:
1. Sorting and Classifying
2. Reading Stories
3. Geometry Patterns
4. Number Patterns
5. Choosing the Example
6. Using Tables

Notes

Students use the strategies practiced in the first six units to solve the problems in this review unit. Specific directions are given for each problem or group of problems.
The exercises on page 24 review Sorting and Classifying.
The exercises on page 25 review Reading Stories.
The exercises on page 26 review Geometry Patterns and Number Patterns.
The exercises on page 27 review Choosing the Example and Using Tables.

Unit 8: Using Pictures
Objective

Use pictures to help understand and solve problems.

Notes

Students see that pictures are a helpful device for solving problems.

The first two pages of this unit provide experiences to help the students use pictures in solving problems. On page 28, students are to match the picture with the word problem. On page 29, students are to use the provided picture to help solve each problem.

Students are to draw their own pictures to help solve the problems on the last two pages of this unit. Simple representations of objects should be encouraged so students don't spend too much time on detailed drawings.

Unit 9: Guessing and Testing
Objective

Find a solution to a problem by guessing a possible solution and testing it to check the accuracy. Improve each subsequent guess based on results of the previous one.

Notes

Throughout this unit students attempt to find the solutions to the problems by making a good guess. If it is found to be incorrect after testing, a better guess is made based on the accuracy of the first guess.

Students should be encouraged to make a reasonable guess (estimate) to start. Each subsequent guess should bring the student closer to the correct answer.

Unit 10: Two Steps
Objective

Use two arithmetic steps to solve a problem.

Notes

Each of the problems in this unit require two arithmetic steps to reach a solution. The steps may involve addition, subtraction, multiplication, or division in any order.

Students should be encouraged to take one step at a time.

Unit 11: Too Much Information
Objective

Find the information to solve a problem.

Notes

The exercises in this unit encourage students to practice their previously learned sorting skills.

On page 40, students distinguish the geometric figures asked about, isolate them from any others, and then count them.

The exercises on page 41 ask students to classify as well as determine what is not needed. They are to write the letter of the fact that is not needed in order to answer each problem.

Students are asked to write the letter of the fact that is not needed in order to answer each problem on page 42.

On page 43, students are to solve the problems by mentally deciding which facts are needed and which facts are not.

Unit 12: More than One Question
Objective

Solve problems with more than one question.

Notes

Each page in this unit consists of a pictograph and a number of questions about that pictograph.

Because the symbols on the pictographs represent more than one object, students are encouraged to use a variety of strategies to answer the problems. The important point is that they answer one question at a time.

Unit 13: Missing Information
Objective

Recognize problems that do not have enough information to be solved.

Notes

On page 46, students are to write the letter of the picture that supplies the needed information for each word problem.

Using the pictures at the top of page 47, students write the missing fact needed to solve each problem.

Students choose the needed fact and write its letter for each problem on page 48.

On page 49, students find the information they need to solve each problem from the chart.

Unit 14: Reasonable Answers
Objective
Check whether or not an answer makes sense.

Notes
By deciding the appropriate operation and estimating the involved numbers, students should be able to arrive at a "close" answer and consequently judge the reasonableness of their calculated answer.

For the exercises in this unit students are asked to write the letter of the answer that makes sense and tell why the other answer does not make sense.

Unit 15: Review Problems
Objective
Review the following problem solving strategies:
1. Sorting and Classifying
2. Reading Stories
3. Geometry Patterns
4. Number Patterns
5. Choosing the Example
6. Using Tables
8. Using Pictures
9. Guessing and Testing
10. Two Steps
11. Too Much Information
12. More than One Question
13. Missing Information
14. Reasonable Answers

Notes
Exercises on page 54 review Geometry Patterns, Number Patterns and Choosing the Example.

Exercises on page 55 review Using Tables, Guess and Test, Missing Information and Reasonable Answers.

Exercises on page 56 review Using Pictures, Guessing and Testing and Two Steps.

Exercises on page 57 review Too Much Information, More Than One Question, Missing Information and Reasonable Answers.

Answers

ANSWERS

UNIT 1

Page 2   **1.** c   **2.** b   **3.** c   **4.** c   **5.** d   **6.** b   **7.** d   **8.** a

Page 3   **1.** f   **2.** e   **3.** b   **4.** a   **5.** d

Page 4   **1.** c   **2.** a   **3.** c   **4.** d   **5.** d

Page 5   **1.** c   **2.** b   **3.** a   **4.** d   **5.** b

UNIT 2

Page 6   **1.** D, A, C, B   **2.** D, C, B, A   **3.** C, D, B, A

Page 7   **1.** D, E, C, A, B   **2.** D   **3.** C   **4.** fourth   **5.** C, A, E, D, G, B, C

        7. E   **8.** B   **9.** F   **10.** second

Page 8   **1.** A   **2.** B   **3.** C   **4.** A   **5.** C

Page 9   **1.** 14   **2.** 7   **3.** 21   **4.** 14   **5.** 25

UNIT 3

Page 10   **1.**   **2.**   **3.**   **4.**

        5. 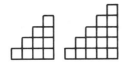   **6.**   **7.**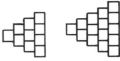

Page 11   **1.** 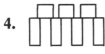   **2.**   **3.**

        4.   **5.**

        6.

UNIT 4

Page 12   **1.** 9, **12, 15, 18, 21**, 24   **2.** 2, 6, **10, 14**, 18, 22

        3. 1, **3, 6, 10, 15, 21**   **4.** 21, **28**, 26, **33**, 31, 38

        5. 34, **35, 37, 38**, 40, 41   **6.** 178, **173, 183**, 178, **188**, 183

        7. 200, **210, 230, 260, 300, 350**   **8.** 20, **21, 19, 22**, 18, 23

Page 13   **1.** 5, 10, 15, **20, 25, 30, 35** Add 5.

        2. 11, 22, **33, 44**, 55, **66, 77** Add 11.

        3. 67, 56, 45, **34, 23, 12, 12**, 1 Subtract 11.

        4. 14, 9, 15, 10, 16, **11, 17, 12** Subtract 5. Add 6.

        5. 41, 38, 35, **32, 29, 26**, 23, **20** Subtract 3.

        6. 60, 68, 63, 71, **66, 74, 69, 77** Add 8. Subtract 5.

Page 14 **1.** 86, 92, 98, **104**, **110**, **116**, **122**, **128** **2.** 100, 104, **108**, 112, **116**, **120**, **124**, **128**
3. 71, 61, **51**, 41, **31**, **21**, 11, 1 **4.** 16, 24, **32**, **40**, 48, **56**, **64**, **72**
5. 100, 91, 83, 76, **70**, **65**, **61**, 58 **6.** 24, 26, 25, 27, 26, **28**, **27**, **29**
7. 5, 10, 20, 25, **35**, **40**, **50**, 55 **8.** 60, 61, 64, 65, **68**, **69**, **72**, **73**
9. 95, 90, 92, 87, **89**, **84**, **86**, 81 **10.** 52, 53, 51, 54, **50**, **55**, 49, **56**

Page 15 **1.** 2, 4, 6, 8, 10, 12, 14, 16, 18, 20 There are 20 shoes altogether.
2. 4, 8, 12 There are 12 rackets in all.
3. 10, 20, 30, 40 There are 40 pencils in all.
4. 5, 10, 15, 20, 25, 30, 35, 40 Julie has 40 pennies.
5. 3, 6, 9, 12, 15, 18, 21 There are 21 plants in all.
6. 5, 10, 15, 20 There are 20 crayons in all.
7. 3, 6, 9, 12, 15 There are 15 balls altogether.
8. 6, 12, 18 There are 18 paint brushes in all.

UNIT 5

Page 16

1.
$$15$$
$$+\ 3$$
18 in all

2.
$$59$$
$$-47$$
12¢ more

3.
$$38$$
$$-\ 7$$
31 are left

4.
$$21$$
$$-12$$
9 are left

5.
$$45$$
$$-27$$
18 more

6.
$$24$$
$$+36$$
60 in all

Page 17

1.
$$53$$
$$+38$$
91
There are 91 beads in the necklace.

2.
$$160$$
$$-\ 85$$
75
Mary has 75 more stamps.

3.
$$94$$
$$+87$$
181
The baker sold 181 cupcakes.

4.
$$82$$
$$-57$$
25
The difference is 25.

5.
$$145$$
$$-\ 78$$
67
There are 67 male goldfish.

6.
$$89$$
$$+66$$
155
The sum is 155.

7.
$$76$$
$$-59$$
17
Kathy has 17¢ more.

8.
$$150$$
$$-\ 93$$
57
57 more planes took off.

Page 18

1.
$$26$$
$$-17$$
9 more

2.
$$26$$
$$+17$$
43 in all

3.
$$43$$
$$+25$$
68 together

4.
$$43$$
$$-25$$
18 more

74

5.	56	6.	56	7.	34	8.	34
	+45		−45		−19		+19
	101 in all		11 more		15 more		53 on both

9.	87	10.	87	11.	90	12.	90
	−73		+73		+68		−68
	14 more		160 together		158 in all		22 more

Page 19

1.	90	2.	90	3.	90	4.	90
	30		−30		−60		+60
	+60		60 more		30 more		150 seeds
	180 in all						

5.	58	6.	58	7.	105	8.	105
	−27		+27		− 27		− 58
	31 more		85 people		78 people		47 people

UNIT 6

Page 20 **1.** 6 **2.** 5 **3.** 14

Page 21 **1.** 31 **2.** grade 5 **3.** 6 **4.** 28 **5.** There are the same amount. **6.** 58
7. 96 **8.** 205

Page 22 **1.**

Cookies	Mrs. Sellinger's Class	Mr. Wood's Class
Chocolate chip	60	36
Peanut butter	82	76

2. 112 **3.** 96 **4.** Mrs. Sellinger's class **5.** 6 **6.** 40 **7.** 24 **8.** 254

Page 23 **1.**

People	Wednesday	Thursday	Friday	Saturday
adults	39	15	47	40
children	52	32	27	63

2. 74 **3.** children **4.** 84 **5.** 174 **6.** 141 **7.** 25 **8.** 315

UNIT 7

Page 24 **1.** b **2.** a **3.** c **4.** c
Page 25 **1.** C, E, A, D, F, B **2.** C **3.** D **4.** fifth **5.** 7 **6.** 168 **7.** 9
Page 26 **1.**   **2.**  **3.**

4. 132, 129, 126, **123**, **120**, 117, **114**, 111   **7.** 8, 16, 24 There are 24 chocolates.

5. 60, 70, 65, 75, 70, **80**, **75**, **85**   **8.** 5, 10, 15, 20, 25, 30, 35, 40, 45 He has 45¢.

6. 3, 4, 6, 9, 13, **18**, **24**, **31**   **9.** 4, 8, 12, 16, 20 wheels altogether.

Page 27   **1.** 8   **2.** 156   **3.** 18   **4.** 31   **5.** 4   **6.** apple   **7.** 2

UNIT 8

Page 28   **1.** c   **2.** a   **3.** e   **4.** b   **5.** d

Page 29   **1.** 5 tickets   **2.** 7 plants   **3.** 7 cookies   **4.** 4 cups

5. 2 nickels, 1 dime, and 2 quarters   **6.** 2 hammers and 7 nails

Page 30   **1.** $6 \times 3 = 18$. There are 18 sides.   **2.** $4 \times 4 = 16$. There are 16 sides.

3. $8 \times 3 = 24$. There are 24 crayons.   **4.** $9 \times 8 = 72$. There are 72 tiles.

5. $3 \times 6 \times 2 = 36$. There are 36 stripes.

Page 31   **1.** 13 marbles   **2.** 11 cookies   **3.** 42 matches   **4.** 12 trees

5. 6 pickets   **6.** 30 minutes   **7.** 1 h 50 min

UNIT 9

Page 32   **1.** 14 and 6   **2.** 24 and 11   **3.** 46 and 17   **4.** 61 and 27   **5.** A = 2, B = 4   **6.** A = 9, B = 7   **7.** A = 5, B = 0   **8.** A = 3, B = 8   **9.** A = 5, B = 2   **10.** A = 3, B = 7

Page 33   **1.** $25 + 10 + 7 + 3 + 0 = 45$ **2.** $10 + 10 + 10$ **3.** $10 + 10 + 7 + 3$ **4.** $25 + 10 + 10 + 7 = 52$ **5.** 1 quarter, 4 nickels, and 2 pennies

Page 34   **1.** one solution is: 2 cars and 1 bicycle   **2.** one solution is: 3 cars and 1 unicycle   **3.** one solution is: 5 cars, 1 bicycle, and 1 unicycle   **4.** one solution is: 4 cars   **5.** 4 squares   **6.** 2 squares and 3 triangles   **7.** 5 triangles   **8.** 4 rectangles and 3 triangles

Page 35   **1.** milk and cheese   **2.** 3 bananas   **3.** 4 bags of peanuts   **4.** 1 banana or 1 apple   **5.** 8 apples   **6.** milk and peanuts   **7.** 2 bags of peanuts and 1 cheese   **8.** milk   **9.** answers vary

UNIT 10

Page 36   **1.** 21 people   **2.** 5 pieces

Page 37   **3.** 20 fish   **4.** 17 cups   **5.** 20 stamps   **6.** 57¢   **7.** 10 min   **8.** 25 cm

Page 38   **1.** 36 names   **2.** 96 envelopes   **3.** 61 boxes   **4.** 61 tickets   **5.** 272 lbs   **6.** 118 children

Page 39   **1.** 21¢   **2.** 54¢   **3.** 3 stickers   **4.** 6 whistles   **5.** 20¢   **6.** 27¢   **7.** 16¢

UNIT 11

Page 40   **1.** 8 squares   **2.** 7 triangles   **3.** 6 circles   **4.** 6 triangles   **5.** 10 rectangles

Page 41   **1.** b, c   **2.** a, d   **3.** c, d   **4.** a, b   **5.** c, d

Page 42   **1.** b and d, 99 in.   **2.** b and c, 46 more children   **3.** c and d, 962 mi   **4.** b and c, 45 baby snakes   **5.** c and d, 36 leaves

Page 43   **1.** $3.24   **2.** 80 minutes   **3.** 13 fish   **4.** 9 years   **5.** 364 fruit trees   **6.** 457 people

UNIT 12

Page 44 **1.** 45 nails **2.** 25 nails **3.** 30 nails **4.** 15 nails **5.** 55 nails **6.** Cory
7. 100 nails
Page 45 **1.** Evelyn **2.** 6 books **3.** 22 books **4.** 10 books **5.** 30 books
6. 44 books **7.** 4 books

UNIT 13

Page 46 **1.** d **2.** e **3.** a **4.** c **5.** b
Page 47 **1.** 3 **2.** 8 rolls **3.** 7 screws **4.** 9 nails **5.** 8 plugs **6.** 6 balls
Page 48 **1.** a, 5 marbles **2.** b, 2 records **3.** a, 2 flowers **4.** a, 3 letters
5. b, Sylvia **6.** b, 7 cm
Page 49 **1.** 16 bears **2.** 3 ducks **3.** 4 cages **4.** 4 cages **5.** 25 squirrels
6. 4 monkeys

UNIT 14

Page 50 **1.** b, 3 km is not enough.
Page 51 **2.** b, 30 students is too small. **3.** a, 50 muffins is too much.
4. b, 300 people is too many. **5.** a, $9.00 is too much.
6. b, 750 jellybeans is too much. **7.** a, 10 decals is too few.
Page 52 **1.** b, $7.00 is not enough. **2.** a, $1.00 is too much.
3. b, 20 m is too short. **4.** b, 30 m is too short.
5. a, 20 minutes is too little.
Page 53 **6.** b, $13.80 is too much. **7.** a, 5¢ is not enough.
8. b, 9¢ is too much. **9.** a, 5 lbs is too little.
10. a, 4 lbs is not enough. **11.** b, 0.3 ft is too short.

UNIT 15

Page 54 **1.**

2. 30, 34, 32, 36, **34, 38,** 36, **40**
3. 15 diamonds
4. 34 + 29, 63 children
5. 34 − 29, 5 children more
Page 55 **6.** 45 children **7.** 18 children more **8.** 28 children more
9. 40 and 12 **10.** 53 and 22 **11.** b **12.** b
Page 56 **1.** 8 dogs **2.** 30 spots **3.** 2 quarters, 3 dimes, and 1 penny **4.** fries
and pie **5.** hamburger and soda **6.** fries and a hamburger
7. 15 boxes **8.** $10.10
Page 57 **9.** 16 people more **10.** 70 bottle caps **11.** 30 bottle caps **12.** 20 bottle caps more **13.** 8 pipe cleaners **14.** 3 bags **15.** a